I0426676

INCOGNITO
(POETRY MANIFEST)

POETRY MANIFEST

BY

VERLENA SEXTON-WALKER

© 2003 by Verlena Sexton-Walker. All rights reserved.

No part of this book may be reproduced, stored in a retrieval system, or transmitted by any means, electronic, mechanical, photocopying, recording, or otherwise, without written permission from the author.

ISBN: 1-4140-0040-5 (e-book)
ISBN: 1-4140-0039-1 (Paperback)

This book is printed on acid free paper.

1stBooks - rev. 07/1/03

Let us discuss how to judge how long one will live by occurrences of body transformation, metamorphosis, transcending, and abnormalities in the environment we live in.

An Old Native American Sacred Spiritual Belief is that during sleep {if} it seems as if you are falling in a hole, count how many times this happens; multiply it by the Biblical terms of life expectancy {3 scores and 10} deriving at your life expectancy in the world and/or the spiritual world. When done, you must analysis yourself and [emphasize on] how close you are to God.

Even in winning you can be defeated. No defeat can be documented as a win unless you truly have the knowledge of what is at risk {as far as winning and losing is concern}...

Mama's Kitchen

I smell collar greens
Black eyed peas
Pinto Beans
In the kitchen that Mama kept
Without Papa's help

I taste apple pie
Cinnamon Rye
In a cake that Mama bake
For Papa's sake

I touch a silk kitchen towel
Chicken foul
In the kitchen that Mama kept
Did Papa help

I sight a cat at play
Mitten lay
In a cake that Mama bake
For Papa's sake

I hear a shout of haste
What a waste
In the kitchen that Mama kept
Papa help
Baking a cake that Mama make
For all sake

Notation is made to [my] personal surroundings so that one can grasp what idiosyncrasies are and how to adjust to them...Living around people that utilize a continuous line of unacceptable norms that they maintain as ones' own by trying to implant them in another' life is call an idiosyncrasy in that no one wants to be like you nor is the person you trying to make jealous of you give a damn about what you do and how you do it...This is called shortcomings because when one goes out to the extreme for attention and still is not being notice appropriately than whom giving you strength - another fool like you...

Finding justification for what is done negatively/wrongly toward another person only says that reality never will be a key factor in all of this——only a false adherent to an inevitable lost through life or death...

Why rock the boat when it is already sinking?

Idiosyncrasies

The brightness of the light
The dimness of the moon
The capacity of child
That grows up to soon

To accomplish the truth
We must get to the root
Illustrating a point of fame
That depletes shame

The shadow in the trees
The humming of the bees
Shows a movement of knowledge
That does not misleads

3

To accomplish the truth
We must get to the root
Illustration of fame
Depleting shame

A state of insanity
Make believe
That all is well
If we deceive

To accomplish the truth
We must get to the root
Point of fame
Depletes shame

Jealous [y]

Beauty in face
Lovely eyes
Disgrace

Exemplified speech
White teeth
Mosaic

Knowledge in walk
The way you talk
Mistake

Persona is your Persona
Who would wanna
Be you
The damn fool that says this is not true

When in correspondence with nature and your surroundings, observation is a key factor in the development of thoughts as will as beliefs that will be lifelong concepts as well as principles.

How to overcome shortcomings and idiosyncrasies in life is truly base on the concept of improving your outer you as well as your spiritual you.

To look within one inner spirit one has to perpetuate an outer spirit that is not only pleasing to oneself but to the environment that one lives within in which this is not an injustice to oneself but helps to eliminate a deluded mind in which happiness is proclaimed—the plush of living that is more than justified toward your concept of what happiness is and should be...

In reference to the above statement, a scenario needs to be created...

To exemplify a continuous line of deceit and atria motives that seems to be one disgusted toward why does she writes and to always try to get your point in first seems to be the your alternative to not facing reality and not being able to say I am living a lie because—all to risk and nothing to gain why not take the risk and be in a continuous line of pain... {Senseless}

Comprehension is to those that know no one should be as stupid as to think they're superior to reality because whomever she desires {only a deluded mind would have the knowledge of not truly knowing} seems to transpire (is she a liar in the truth is not in her)...
A woman {unraveling} has designated an injustice to what is appropriate and what is not appropriate...
Whom does she hate...? The person she thinks she is winning against...I feel extremely sad when referring to this State and the [dimness] within it...

Intelligence is the character within knowledge in which justifications of all things are for real and not for fake...

When you are 'rich' everything else seems nonsense and refinement to the concept of foolishness and disgust...

The World of Imagination

Magnificent is the world of imagination
Prognosis of hesitation

Detroit city limits is where I am at
With a forty ounce in my hand and money to bet
Every night I am in a bar
Gambling with fixed cards
The money I win is mine to keep
Not spending none on my women—only on me

In the mind of an addict I sleep
Addicting him as he creeps
Only dealing with the metropolitan man
Who holds a crack pipe in his left pocket in his 'right' hand

Taking money from his family
He slips into make believe
Arrested by the police
He doesn't even have shoes on his feet

Magnificent is the world of imagination
Prognosis of hesitation

Complaints

My head is tired
Lay it down
My face is sore
Why you frown
My feet feel funny
Are they numb
No money in my pocket
That's call a bum

Complaints are something we shouldn't say
Working our way through a day

My mother fusses
All the time
My coat is torn
Can you rhyme
My hand hangs awkward
Retardation
My speech sometimes slurs
Lord, my word

Complaints are something we shouldn't tell
Moving away from a pavilion known as hell

I am autistic
The fool would share
When whom he's telling does not care

Again, my teeth are double
Close your damn mouth
My eyes are crossed
Sit down on the couch

My toe is swollen
Soak your feet
The key to this is turned indiscreet

Complaints are cries that no one hears
Essence of damnation and what we hold in a tear
Adding on is prolongation of fear

Complaints are something we shouldn't share
Creating a passage that asks "Do I care?"

What in the World

Exotic she is called
In appearance
Beautiful she is seen
Behind a screen
Dancing on a stage
That cultivates the body
Placing the mind in a daze

Associate this to nothing
And you will get something

I have the figure she boasts
The shape of what—a hostess
Coming through a motor of car
Does your remembrance go that far

Associate this to nothing
You will get something

Walking up the stairs as fast as she can
Stomping while saying I'm gonna win
Did Pooh put her pussy in your face
The epitome of disgrace

Associate this to nothing
Again, you will get something

Placing hands on her hips
Talking in tips
Thinking all that is written is about her
Illicit, explicit, picking up the fur

Associate this to nothing
Just once, you will get something

Your Name Is What

Is it the name that catches your attention
Did I mention
That I was given this name at birth
Did that hurt

Are you whom you say you are
Can your mind go that far

I know whom you where when we 'first' met
You wanna bet
Only thing you knew is what you did
Is that why you wear a wig

Are you whom you say you are
Expand the mind
Let's talk in this bar

Television has move into a new millennium
Taking over the body one by one
Why would you want to be me when I don't want to be you
I see what is to be true

Are you whom you say you are
What do I have to do - take the bar

Attorneys, Lawyers at work
Making sure I get fuck
To much money for you to have
Why do you want to share
Knowledge to a nobody

Are you whom you say you are
At birth I was given this name
Again, are you whom you say you are
Negative, I have given you the answer thus far

A journey {wrong or right} in life that has been more than twice is called by some an ignominy to mankind and you should become despondent afraid of disgrace because who want a monkey trying to keep pace...Give up living so it can be a personal victory {you}.?. How untrue. Who says that you should always feel a win when the only thing you are winning is an inevitable ending to a man running after [ass] as if it is his last...? Stand up and be notice because if there a such thing as an immortal damn fool with utilization of a [twisted]concept/belief in oneself as a tool to bring harm, pain, and shame to end a so called game - let the man tip his hat and have the fame...

In the Mind of Millions

Swinging from a tree
Does not mean a damn thing to me
All I see is a dominant form of insanity

Capturing a thought
Fought
In a dream
Scheme

Yelling to top of your voice
Is your choice
Making a difference
Not even once

Capturing a thought
Fought
In a scheme
Dream

Raising your hand in the air
As if you don't care
Illustrating a stupid stunt
You the bunt

Thinking of fighting
Thought
Capturing strength
Fought
In a dream
Scheme

Living more than a decade in this psychotic masterpiece called the world. Let us picture this. Moses wrote The Ten Commandments on a mountain with a tool God made for him to carve writing into stone. He put those writings in the Holy Scripture called the Bible. Immaculate...Just a simple example of something that was at one time complex but is not anymore. The idea behind this passage is that god tells us that there is no such quotation of something being unspoken when it is for righteousness/justice for once something is done an than repeated, it will become accessible to discussion as well as disgust.

Visualization

Picture this...
If that was gorgeous
Would you adore her
With a personality that sucks
Would you still want to fuck - her

Visualization is everything
It can bring joy and pain
As well as make you mundane

Accomplishment of a goal
Distinguish
Make you a well player in the business sense
Eventually becomes past tense

Visualization is something
It can be the difference in win or lose
You choose

Each time I report a fault
What lesson have I taught
Only the intelligent is willing to learn
A comedian having fun

Visualization is many things
Difficulties in a theme
Surely will acquire a dream
Do I plot or scheme

Virtual Reality

Are you who I see in the door
Would this be a love look or do you adore
Does it appear to be the look of hate
Your emotions are fake

Reality becomes virtuality when not plan
It's your chose
Be a man

Sitting at the table in the center of the floor
I decided to take no more
The waitress is ignoring me for others
Tapping the bell asking her what's the trouble

Reality becomes virtuality when you take a stand
With a dominant aura that is within your talk
Depicting you the man

The scenario goes as such
Which would you chose
The yellow back of deceit
The strength in discreet

Reality becomes virtuality even if plan
It's anyone chose
Be a man
The potency of a woman is in her stance
Giving her a better chance

Reality becomes virtuality when well done
The sun doesn't shine just for you to have fun

Perception

Blight
Fight
Which is right

A man standing on the street asking for something to eat
A women passing by, a tear dropping from her eye
Indian way to fame to accomplish shame

Blight
Fight
Which is right

A drunk staggering
An addicted fanatic
Black way of shame to accomplish fame

Blight
Fight
Which is right

A suicidal cry
A molestation try
White way of shame to accomplish fame

Blight
Fight
Which is right

An organize crime
A taste of the finest wine
Italian way to fame to accomplish shame

Blight
Fight
Which is right

Disfigurement in a brawl
Perspective of a crawl
Any way of shame to accomplish fame

Blight
Fight
This is right

50 years from now another movement/violation will effect/affect someone life because some fools wants to be famous in both lives - rich and common (not rich)...Stupidity in its highest...Tomorrow is everyday...Each state will have a different form of expression...But all will be for the same purpose——to rob, steal, and kill...None that can be equivalent to Satanic verses...

Why would a person call you when they tell you not to call them? I live around ignorant people that reality will never befriend...Admiration toward repetitious of something that can not nor will not happen again...

When you are on a journey toward a new millennium in life as if you have lived through wars, famine, and unbelief's, you take these life gifts and facilitate them as if they are the Holy Scripture...God has truly given you insight to what is not right but can never be Satanic...Technology is manmade...Anything made by man can only develop falsities to what is real and what is unreal. When attempting to destroy, talk to God - not to man. In reason, the only way indecency can be taken out of ones life is when you are indecent and continue to believe that person have love for you (keep your enemies close, however, not as close as your next door neighbor).

Eclipse

Toot
Blow
The sound of a horn

Fax machine
On top of a car

Rapping
Singing
Walking Mack

Fax machine
In my back

Laughing
Talking
All in one

Fax machine
Says I'm number one

The simple attack through technology
Is despicable to me

Fax machine on top of a car
Yelling, "you knew" from afar
Reminds me of all that is lost
Knowledge of knowing who will pay the cost

Common Sense

Struggling to accomplish the improbable
Acquiring what is possible
Means you look at things with inaccurate vision
Indecision

Knowledge comes from what is learned
Sharing is a concept
When all is given and nothing is received
What knowledge can you achieve

Covetousness is the eyes
Dipology of disguise
When one beauty shines through
Play who

Knowledge comes from what is learned
Caring is a concept
When you show love but it is not in return
What knowledge have you earned

Minor pains are yours now
Just know how
To eliminate verbatim and repetitions
Should not be a difficult feat
Just, remember the people you meet

Knowledge comes from what is learned
Sharing is a concept
In every approach don't accept
Receiving knowledge that is well kept

Old Man Chant

My, my, my
What a beauty
Look at all that booty
Sitting ready to touch
I wonder will she kick me where it hurts

An old man chant
Is a wonderful thing
Bringing back the years as he sings

Hair is jet black
With peachy skin
Her teeth are white
As she grins

An old man chant
Is a sound for the hears
Bringing you close to tears

"My wife look just like that when she was young"
"Her hair was long but she always wore it in a bun"

An old man chant
Is finally over
'I' hope he doesn't get any older

Who Faults Are They

Aunt Estella is her name
She has ways that would make you ashamed
For her that is
She is ill and ready to kill

Why do we find faults in others
Because they are not our sister or brother

Carrie walks with snuff in her mouth
While she cleans up her house
Never married in her life
But always telling you what is right

Why do we find faults in others
Because we have no sisters or brothers

Mary is the slut of the streets
Performing sexual acts of all kinds
Still wanting to be a friend of mine

Why do we find faults in others
Maybe because these are our sisters and brothers

Velma came clean long ago
She was once the class whore
But now everything is right in her life
In essence, does she live without strife

Why do we find faults in others
These are all sisters and brothers

The momentum of this poem
Is not in one
If this is your sister or brother
The damage is done

Again, why do we find faults in others
Let's embrace and be sisters and brothers

Familiarity

Family ties can be far apart
Family ties can be in the heart
When all walk together as one
Family ties have won

Mourning is done at a funeral
In a room of many kin
Depicting who get what in the end

Family ties can be far apart
Family ties can be in the heart
When all walk together
Family ties can become much better

A wedding is held in a cathedral
The priest says, "I now pronounce you husband and wife"
Two months later the marriage is denounced

Family ties can be far apart
Family ties can be in the heart
When all hold hands in unison
Family ties becomes a communion

My mother lay sick in a hospital bed
While hemorrhaging in the head
Rolling his eyes trying not to cry
My father says, "The bitch should die."

Family ties becomes at odds
Family ties have fallen apart
When one wish for an inevitable death
Family ties are gone with nothing left

Does This Make Sense

Past tense should be left that way
Why open old wounds when you have nothing to say
Apologizing becomes awkward

I said you did me wrong than
Now I chose to win
My knowledge is more pertinent now
Winning is only how

Memories of what has been done
Does not tell who has won
Just, the difference between winning and losing

I asked, "Do you know what wrongs are on your slate?"
Do you really know whether I hate
Acceptance of your problems is not for me
You deal with yours and leave me be

Life is current to all that's absolute
The moment of truth
Is within my grasp

I said I did no wrong
Turning you off not on
Apologizing, for what

Actuality

Why you keep trying
You fooling your damn self
I don't like you and you know that

Chooses are chooses
Who told you to choose
You misleading yourself
You'll end up being used

Open your eyes
Brings insight
Noticing it
Will make you alright

Chooses are chooses
Why did you chose
Are you so gullible
Easily confused

Arguments are continuous
And on-going process
Your mouth is hanging open
Senseless

Chooses are chooses
Did you chose
Life is fell with up and downs
Confused

Futile

Coldest as any winter
A man stands along
Recalling his life
Wondering is it gone

Walking around
No where to go
In the middle of the room
Opening a door

The blackest of your eyes
Tells me many things
The chiming of the bells
Still rings

Walking in a pace
No where to go
A man is in a stance
No money to show

Manipulation, are you for real
Who should be ashamed
You the one 'mentally' ill

Police sirens are everywhere
People of this city believe they care

Walking in haste
What for
The sadness is
You are looking for an award
When your life has been placed in a deck of cards

Pretext {Alleged Reason}

The stupidest word I ever heard was dummy
The strangest thing I ever seen was fake money
The wildest girl in the world is my cousin
The crazies' man in the land is my x-husband

Describing the way things are and not how they seem
Brings a picturesque square of why the 'cage birds sings'

The love of beauty
The hate of grace
The plainness of a face

Describing the way the moon sets can be priceless
Bringing knowledge to the mind that surpasses time

The glass house on the hill
Frames a portrait
Of a simple life and each step
It takes to accomplish a dream
While making a dress and hemming the seam

Describing ones imagination can become real
Acquiring a fulfillment beyond years

Within all, all is well
No longer willing to share
In which only brings bad relations
That depletes procrastination

Description is done in many ways
Do we say hallelujah or just praise

You Speak French

Do you see me out in the city at night
You don't be out there and you have lived here all your freaking life

English can ask questions
Poetry is in a simile
Question marks do not have to be

Compare me to whom
For what reason
The saying goes, "For everything there is a season"

English can ask questions
Poetry is in a metaphor
Questions marks, what for
Read this poem and you will want more

Standing on sidelines a football player catches a pass
White man runs on the field and hazes the ass
Does this mean this team will lose
Who will say when they don't play by the rules

English can ask questions
Poetry is in a statement
Questions marks become hesitations

If I asked you for a dollar
Would you say I don't know you that well
A rich man riches signed him into hell

English can ask questions
Poetry is in an exclamation
Does this hesitate you or is this called procrastination

Poetry Manifestation

I had a thought as I was climbing the stairs
A cricket
A bird
A feeling in my hair

This poem will manifest
Reading it will be the test

A man in black exit the bathroom
Believing he was evil and would destroy me soon
Putting my head in his stomach
The words spoken where, "You will be bald"
Making me my cousin after all

This poem will manifest
Reading it is the test

Paper in the white man hand
Deploys a plan
To scare and scar as much as he can
Winning slavery all over again

This poem will manifest
Reading it shouldn't be a test

Purpose is in the project
Lies are utilize
Ones to depict
Ones to despise

This poem will manifest
Reading it is your test

Many lives have been touched
Through crimes of such
Nature that is
Causing a illness in magnitudes
Abused, confused, or misconstrued

This poem will manifest
Reading it is the final test

Gross Point Park

A glisten window that I sat by
Give me insight on why
The things that mankind do
Toward me and you

Don't be afraid I won't bite
We don't have to even fight
The day is created for your defense
Maliciousness is what is meant

A judge gave the verdict
He said dismiss
Question asked come to this
Firstly, I shouldn't had to pay a fine
However, this was not a waste of my time
Enlightenment came in a mist
Reasoning was past tense

Are you afraid I won't bite
Not even put up a fight
Two days have been created to shallow fear
Putting a dot in the ear

A public defender decided first
Saying the judge would take her word
No questions asked
No answer given
The truth to this public defender

You afraid you think I'm gonna bite
It seems as if you want to fight
Three days have been created just for you
To hide behind——misconstrued/miss-used

Aspirations

Fear can come in knowing
Knowledge is your choose
Not knowing can be defermental
Let expression be voiced

When you sing is it in your gut
Is it lovely or does it hurt
When you read how is your pronunciation
Does it flow or is there hesitation

Knowledge is fear of knowing to much
It's your life don't think such
Defermental things happens to fools
Expression is in voice why choose

Innovative ideas can become initiatives
Give
Not your concepts before recognition
Putting them in writing before you even mention

Fear can come in knowing
Knowledge is your choose
Not knowing can be defermental
Expression can be voiced

Many times remembrance slips
When words that should have been spoken
Were moments on your lips

Knowing is knowledge
Why fear
Foolishness deferments
Listen don't hear
When all words have been spoken and enough said
Expression is your knowledge
Are you mislead

Consenting Adult

Dim the lights
Turn on the air
Take the beret out of your hair
Standing in the Foyer of the house
The women began unbuttoning her blouse

This is the first step toward foreplay
I wonder will she get laid

"Now I want you to unfasten my bra."
She said as she step out the car
Entering the house in a haste
She began to pace

This is the second step toward foreplay
I wonder will this just be a trip in the hay

Off came the blouse and the skirt
She held her hand as if it hurt
Tears rolling down her eyes
She turned with a smile
"I'm not a virgin but I'm so scare."
Moving toward the bedroom as she spoke
Whom is she talking to——a ghost

This is the third step toward foreplay
What a waste of time I must say

Sitting on the bed with her mouth open astound
The stranger came in without a sound
Did they make love or just have sex

This is the final step
Foreplay is done
Making love has begun

Military Strategist

Gossiping in the afternoon
Talking about whom
Calling bad names out
Is this is what life is all about

If I said this to her
I surely can say it to you
This is what the truth can do

Her head is bald she wears a wig
Her skin is scaly and they call her big
She is slow
Can't capture a thing
Why does she believe she can sing

If I said this about you behind your back
I can say it to your face as a matter-of-fact

His mother is a drug addict
Neglecting her children because of her fanatics
His daddy drinks corn whiskey by the jugs
Not supporting or showing love

If I said this about your family in your face
Does that not tells where you are place

All the things that is vicious
Can become malicious
Guarding your tongue is not the key
Giving victory that shouldn't be

Justified

Just began
Just first
Just start
Just end
Just as you think
You will win

Who do you think that white man is
Nothing but a wanna be Indian
Who doesn't know how to kill

Just an accomplishment
Of a goal
When do you think you will be old
Just an overachiever
Letting you in
Don't began celebrating before you win

Who do you think that black man is
Nothing but a wanna be Indian
Who is willing to kill

Just a remembrance
Of what we once had
Not even a victory
I got the last laugh

Who do you think that Indian man is
A wanna be black man in white man skin
Feeling sadness that surpasses the years
A mental warpath the can 'never' be healed

Mack Avenue

The noise outside is so loud
A child stands along in the crowd
People are fighting over whom should lead
When the leader will not succeed

If I was out there in that crowd
I would break it up beginning with the child
From point of attack I would know what to do
Depicting whom is the biggest damn fool

These people think this is a sign of fear
The joy is in the eyes and the voices I hear
They scream at the bedroom window I am in
As if they are caged animals in a pen

If I was congested in that crowd
I would break the barrier because I know how
Forming a point of attack from the start
Showing them that this is not very smart

Out of all I see, a man sticks out
Letting me know what he is all about
His skin is hasten and dusty to
He seems as if he doesn't know what to do
This man began to laugh senseless
The sound is in pretense
He turns to me to hold a conversation
I walk away without hesitation

If the crowd began to grow smaller
You will know why
Separating the means from the reasons
With a loud shout
Letting them know what I'm all about
Scaring everyone in the streets
This is an accomplishment that lacks defeat

Designation

Surely be glad when you do that
Accomplished anything yet
Stay criminal without education
Amazing

Ideas can be a great thought
Though the minds of children that aren't taught
Right from wrong early in life
Never learning to think twice

You can't help me
Seems as if I am helping you
In every poem there's a fool
Any man attics is for him to be proud of
Is this what you call love

Inventions are creation of the mind
Can become great developments in time
However, if they are not to help but hinder
It could become a finder bender
In all is well says a wise man
While taking money out of my hand
Comes up short change
Believes that this was arranged

Creations are a designer tool
These definitions were taught in school
Deciding which one to use
Is truly 'left' up to you

Signifies the Significant

You do
Drop directly between my legs
And think you getting in my head
I do to

The signals on a car is always yellow
Does this make you mellow
Zoning a girl before womanhood
If only you could

"Who want her?" Shouts a man
A prize monkey is the plan
God made us in his 'own' image
Does this even make you timid

The signals says which way to turn
You are not the only the one
Monkeys come out in a magnitude
Prize monkeys are always used

"You skink." Says the man
Great apes are cookies in a can
God made us in his splitting image
Please not let this make you timid

"You knew." Says the woman
Animal crackers are good to
In your first life you lived as a frog
Reasoning after all
Dissecting you is in a book
Changing you to the human look

VERLENA SEXTON-WALKER

The signals are now turn off
Getting out the car
Walking in the house
Not that far
When will they ever change the color
When yellow is the only one and there is no other

Buoyancy

Telling you the things I can do
I will take your man from you
Doesn't this sound like confidence
This is the future not past tense

Fix your hair
Dress yourself
Make-up your face
Look your best

Let me ask you a few questions
Do you see yourself as beautiful
A woman that any man would adore
This confidence you have is misconstrued
  You are subject to being used

Fix your eyelashes
They are falling off
Wipe your mouth
With this cloth
Dress yourself in your sharpest attire
Than you be ready to walk down the aisle

  Again, I have all the confidence in the world
Every man tells me I'm a beautiful girl
  Not to late to take some advice
  How about showing what you call "doing it right."
  The eyelashes should be just like that
The lipstick shouldn't be blood red
  And never walk around with a comb in your head
Men desire a woman who dress smart
  This is the place you should start

VERLENA SEXTON-WALKER

Fix your hair
Dress yourself
Make-up your face
Look your very best

To Began With—I Don't Want To Walk

Explicit Illicit the hole they create
Through the irony of pain in what we call hate
This is the dialogue of a man walking along
Wondering around trying to find his way home

A journey of the mind is better in a group
Why walk along when I'll walk with you

Is nudity crudity when there is disfigurement of the body
Beauty is in the eye of the beholder
Why bother
To say I like my man or woman with a shape
When love is the only thing that depletes hate

A journey in time develops memory
Associate this evaluation while researching history

Modest the Goddess that sits next to me
Talking about how graceful she will be
Forgetting the story of Pinocchio
Her nose began to grow

A journey that is not plan in life
Can become tiresome to any man and full of strife

An image is a picture of a role model
That can become your genie in a bottle
Idolizing can be a mistake
Watch the chooses you make

A journey in life is ready to began
What do you think you will accomplish in the end

Cuff Her

Sirens all around
People lying on the ground
A bomb exploded next door
Evacuation was slow

In the middle of the streets a woman stands
With cuffs around her hands
Not knowing why
Tears falling from her eyes

"Cuff her" is screamed
Because of this
Self-destruction is the result
Not pointing the finger at whose fault

This is not a black and white world
There are many races
Why the protruding eyes and the ugly faces

In the hall stands a man with drugs in his mouth
Police surrounds him telling him to spit them out
Putting cuffs around his wrist
The scene escalates
Taking manhood from a man in a neighborhood of hate

"Cuff her" is screamed
Because of this
Self-destruction is the result
Not pointing the finger at whose fault

Reality tells us what they want us to believe
In which a damn is not given
If all is well and nothing on
What than went wrong

In a police car sits a mother and child
Laughing from afar is heard from a market stand
The mother sees many things with cuffs around her hands
This is what the white man calls a dominant plan

"Cuff her" is screamed
Because of this
Self-destruction is the result
Not pointing the finger at whose fault

Within all scenarios are messages
Let's decide on the lessons
Do you respect the police
Even when they are deceit
Is corruption a choice
Don't you have a voice

"Cuff her" is screamed
Because of this
Result—Self-destruction
This is present not past tense

EXPLOSION!!!

Darkness

In my life I have been misconstrued
Misconceptions—Misused
Not the subject abuse
Whom to know what is true

How can you balance life
When you see through others eyes
Connecting things of their reality
Monologues lives and gravity

A maze is in the mind
Depicting and Depleting time
In which everything is fine
The glisten shines
Through imprudence that is
Changing sick into ill

How can you think everything is alright
Is this an act
When you see things through two set of eyes
Hate becomes undisguised

Money ruins people
All is well if you are rich
Standing on a stifle
Are you ready for this

How
Is all I have to say
Let's just end it this way

Basketball

Driving in the city today with my windows down
The freeway is clear
Should I leave this town

What's all that commotion I hear in these city limits
People with intense fear
The matrix of a menace

Waving at whom I know
Not that many
In the absence of friendship
Can I find any

What's all that commotion I hear in these city limits
Children are playing in the streets
The matrix of a menace

Clapping at the enjoyment I see
Passing by
A man in a clown suit
Swatting a fly

The city limits of Detroit is where I am at
Commotion continues to be heard
Nothing more to say about that
A matrix of a menace has been created
Is this jealousy or am I just hated

Prota Call

Attention getter
I am surely that
People fall over things just to call me fat

Notice me
Can you resist
Even if I could
It would be in pretense
And misunderstood

If this is what you call your concept
Keep it to yourself and get some help

Brown eyes, Brownish hair, light complexion
Does this profile brings complication
The horn of an eighteen wheeler just blowed
All over a piece a pussy that's old and cold

Why you come through my back
You really think this makes me you
I have never cleaned out a camole or a toilet stool

If this is what you call your concept
Keep it to yourself
And before you finish—please get some help

How much life is given to us
If any
Count your nickels and dimes and hold on to your pennies

You really want to walk in my shoes
I'm not that old
When you snatch something out of my hand
You've been told

A wise man once told a story about the seven seas
When he finish he said, "This is make believe."

Why you come through my back
I know you really want to be me
I always taught in occupation
Janitorial duties are not foreseen

Euphoria

Melodies in the air
The wind blows in my hair
Standing by a handsome man
At a donut stand

This is a scene
Not for real
This happens every year

Children on the playground
Laughter all around
Sitting on a bench in the park
A blanket lying in a yard

This is a scene
Not for real
Happening every year

Man and woman embracing
Painting chocolate faces
Cheerleaders yelling for their team
All in a dream

These are scenes not scenarios
At the picture show
This happens every year
Of course, I'm for real

Disengaged

White pampers with pins
Sadness within
Of the adult whom is now a baby
Because she can't win

Let's have sex
I am so ready
This is voiced

Finger in the mouth
Crying out loud
Is done
When all is said——have you won

Let's make love
I am so emotional

Chest heaving
Sparkling eyes
This is not completed

Living

You appeared in front of me
An image I did not see
Than it change all of a sudden
Why is this meant to be

More than a life to me
I discover
Mine not yours
Or my brothers'

Looking at wood
With protruding eyes
Tell me many things
Do you realize

More than a life to me
I discover
Mine not yours
Or mothers'

Raising the blinds to see outside
A man is passing by with hate in his eyes
Knowing the reason is because I won't give-up my life
To the ugly woman he calls his wife

More than a life to me
I discover
Laying in my bed reaching for cover
Everyone wants my life for their own
Or is this just a spirit telling me what is wrong

Exploration

In a third world country
One is told
That life can be very cold

Loneliness is your best friend
The only one you can depend

Darkness comes quick at night
There is not any light

Turning on a lamp
This is how you camp

In a world where there is a marketplace
People move in a haste
Not associating with anyone
Spending money on none

Sun rises early on
The tone is set
As you began thinking about
The people you have met

In a state of a world that is asylum
The stage is set for a fool
Who says this is me
In world that is without principles
And mentality

The sun rises early on
You set the tone
Beginning to think about whom is there
And whom you will meet

All along

Simple

Economics
The world a money
Statistics
Accomplishments

All are subjects of a cheat
Diagramming whom he can beat

Accounting
Numbers game
Financing
Money pain

All are subjects of a cheat
A diagram of whom to beat

Mathematicians these are not
Only idiots that will get caught
In the crunch of false figures
As the prize get bigger and bigger

Knowledge

She knows is continually said
As I lay in my bed
By old folks in this town
Called a city

Vision is in the air
As I set in my chair
Not a word do I say

A coin is drop on the ground
The noise is a quirky sound
As I bend down

Vision is in the air
Mission accomplished
In reason with what is said
As I lay in my bed

Confidentiality is in the house
Playing as if he knows
This is how it unfolds

Vision is in the air
Mission insight
This is the chose you made
Who want to fight

Perennial Aerobics

Hold your hand over your mouth
Let out a shout
Is it muffled in your ear
Or does everyone hear

How do we know when others listen
If we speak not to them

Do it loud as loud as you can
That gets their attention

Raise your hand in the air
As far as they can go
Touch your toes
Rub your nose
All together

How do we know we are on the same beat
Communicate
Cross your arms
Wiggle your feet

Jump up high
Run inside
Is this exercise

Clap your hands
Take a stand
Stop

This will be repeated one more time
Ready
Hop

(DO AS MANY TIMES AS YOU LIKE)

Dominance in Nature

Amazing to see success
With all those obstacles
Is it a thought
Or motivation

A story of a man that has nothing to give
But his time and patience to the mentally ill

A blessing in the making as surely as you live
To help ones that can not help themselves
Is to share and give

A story of a child that walks on crutches
Shows the strength of well
For others

A weakness is not shown through writing
Not even in the eyes that changes for the occasion
Silliness comes in persuasion

A tale of two people doing the same thing
Is a shameful set of events
When in time it's not well spent

A gift is not a gift if it does not come from God
It can be taken so easily
Quickly disregard

A tale finally told of Achilles' heel
A weakness depicted strength
When that man succeeds
Is this finally the ending blessing
That one can give
If this man is the one that is mentally ill

Soaring

Out of the aches American rose
In shambles of old
A story is told
Of living through slavery of control
A 'man' stands hugging a pole
Visionary error foretold
Out of the aches American rose

Many struggles on her slate
That teaches emotions of hate
In a room of disgrace
Is this useless or fate
That puts shame in its place

Out of the aches American rose
In shambles of cold
Victimization or control
Missionary foreseen
That implicit a scene
Out of the aches American rose

Striving through strife
Learning things that were not 'just' right
In a hall of disrespect no regret
Not finish, Not yet

Out of the aches American rose
The shambles unfold
Of victimization as well as violation
Hated
Lack of control
Vision, Mission foretold
Out of the aches American rose

You Know Me…- I Know You…

There's a dominance presence in my place
Still not able to place the face
To recognize says that it should be here
The reality is too much to bear

Is this a symbol of an ending
Maybe a sign of a beginning
Not a spirit of the dead
This person wants my head

"A wimp", I keep hearing in the background
Walking quietly
Not making a sound

Is this symbol of love to come
Or this just tells me I am not the only one
Standing at my bedroom window
I began to ponder

"Pussy", expresses a voice outside
Ignorance that can not hide
Jealous of not knowing

Symbolic is not the word
Signs are seen and not heard
Because of things said
Still trying to sleep in my bed

Who threw their life away
Not I, I must say
The presence has become much stronger

VERLENA SEXTON-WALKER

Symbols are signs for a premonitionist
Not for a futuristic
When signs are signs and symbols are symbols
Who gonna forget
Do you remember

[Reversal]

"You see me", he said out loud.
As he transcend in the house
Not afraid to let you know
I am not a spirit anymore

Why do I transcend in this place
Is it the beauty of her face
Or the knowledge of what to come
Am I not the only one

Pacing back in forward in virtuality

I am the spirit that you see
Horizontal I walk fast
Before the vision has past

Transcending in and out
Beauty in face
Knowledge of an outcome
Am I not the only one

The dominance presence is in place
Still can not place your face
How quickly we give-in
This is the beginning not the end

Youtilize Life

Realize, Recognize, Youtilize Life

In a third world country where it is dark and cold
The young knows what it is to be old
Without hope of a better tomorrow
Escalates sorrow
That depicts the destiny of life
In a country without sacrifice...

A child walks to a pond of water to quiche a thirst
A mother feed baby bread
In the eyes of the people living in a hurdle
Laying on the ground that has no cover
Decides when will this country grow from poverty to feeding the
poor
Is in perspective without a government of a country that can not
take anymore

In a third world country where it is dark and cold
The young knows what it is to be old
Without hope of a better tomorrow
Shadowed with sorrow
Escalates a depicted scene
Destiny of life is the mean
In a country without a sacrificing dream...

One must {began [to]}-

Recognize, Youtilize, Realize life

Verlena Sexton-Walker
05-09-2003

Hair [Undisguised Distrust]

It is not always easy to bring into focus the things that you are aware of that effects/affects your environment as well as your surroundings. People are constantly expressing how they dislike your persona because they cannot obtain it. Jealousy is a word that should be utilized nowadays to describe things that should not be in anyone's' life.

Example:

Hair short
Hair long
When you were bald
I had it going on
Now you wouldn't cut your hair anymore
You continue to let it grow
This makes me have to look at me
And I don't like the women I see
Disassociation of what is true
I'll wear a wig that will help 'me' get through

A woman thinking that hair is what makes another woman beautiful and unique with no desire to be {petite}…

{Rerouting}

Hair short - {STOP}

Hair long - {YIELD}

When you were bald - {ATTENTION}

I had it going on - {HELL}

Now you wouldn't cut your hair anymore -

{BETTER}

You continue to let it grow - {REALITY}

This makes me have to look at me - {NEED}

And I don't like the women I see - {BLESSING}

Disassociation of what is true - {JAMES}

I'll wear a wig that will help 'me' get through - {AUNT SHAME}

EXPLORATION:

A women thinking {AVANT} that hair is what

makes another women beautiful and unique

with no desire to be {petite}...{COMPLETE}

Getting to Know the Author

A book of poetry is always a unique first book to write. It comes from the ultimate depths of your spirit. When writing INCOGNITO {POETRY MANIFEST}, I discovered another realm of the spirit that otherwise would not have been foreseen. This spirit told me that it was time to expand my horizons in a book of poetry. I have written poetry all my life; however, this spirit inspired me to share this gift with others. These poems are poems that convey dominant presence in persona as well as the annotation of life itself.

Being Mississippi born on a hot day in September of 1966, I have seen many things that the end of the Civil Rights Movement says I shouldn't have. In statement this means nothing but in living it could be life or death, happiness or sadness, strength or weakness, and many more odds to ends that have been captured through the color of my skin and the heritage I'm in—Native American.

My great grandmother use to say to me as a child that I had magnificent eyes. Never knowing what this meant by compliment, when she was dying she told me you will be able to see into the future Magnificent Eyes. The future is still unfolding by twenties and not one by one.

"Capture your dominant aura through your own struggles; not ones you create for another/others." VSW Is a personal statement that has stuck with me for years. Saying that when all is false and you utilize others things to make them true in life, fear become undisguised because you are verbalizing that you forgot that capabilities are made; not given.

The opportunity of a life time is not a suggestion but a focus toward many more books of poetry. I hope this book brings you immense enjoyment and capabilities of life not death, happiness not sadness, strength not weakness, and many more ends that will bring inspiration and motivation to you.

VERLENA SEXTON-WALKER
06-12-2003
4:10:10 PM

www.ingramcontent.com/pod-product-compliance
Lightning Source LLC
Chambersburg PA
CBHW020357290526
45785CB00005B/2332

* 9 7 8 1 4 1 4 0 0 0 3 9 8 *